PANBODY BLUES

Abdulai Walon-Jalloh

Sierra Leonean Writers Series

Panbody Blues
Copyright © 2017 by Abdulai Walon-Jalloh
All rights reserved.

ISBN: 978-9988-8697-7-9

Sierra Leonean Writers Series

Panbody Blues
Poems

Dedication

This work is dedicated to all my teachers and friends, and particularly to the memory of Mohamed Conde also known as M.C, and Abdul Rahman Bangura Esq. a practising lawyer. You two have really inspired me to write. Allah bless you.

Acknowledgements

I acknowledge the support of colleagues who have peer-reviewed this work. I appreciate your criticisms, praises and suggestions. Thank you for being frank with me. I thank my friends who have been by my side all this time and who continue to stand by me. To Mallam O, thank you for the encouragement and platform to enable me express myself. To my numerous readers around the world who continue to read, appreciate, critique and inspire me to continue to write. I thank you very much. The Ataya bases around the country have always been my anchor. I recognise your invaluable and spiritual bonding you have offered and continue to provide me. Thank you, brothers and sisters. The media, SLWS, Amazon, Vitabu etc., without whom I would not have been able to reach wider audiences, I doff my hat to you. To my beautiful wife and playful children, thank you for being patient with me as you have overlooked my sometimes exaggerated and eccentric behaviour.

Contents

Acknowledgements, i
Endorsements, v

POEMS

Absence Presence, 1
I'm Badrie, 2
The Loss, 3
God, 4
The Truth, 5
Power, 6
The Passing Stream, 7
Friends and Peace, 8
The Arrival, 9
Binta: The Abyss, 10
Binta: The Anti-climax, 11
Binta: The Pre Anti-climax, 12
Binta: The Climax, 13
Binta: The Sun Sets, 14
Binta: The Dawn, 15
Binta: The Sun Rises, 16
Tomorrow, 17
Yesterday, 18
Today, 19
In Memory of the fallen, 20
Geometry Set in Pain, 22
Ice and Dice, 23
Eid, 24
Poetry, 25

The World in Parts, 26
Brave Cowards, 28
The Sun and the Palm Tree, 29
Dublin, 31
Guardians of the Earth, 33
Robin, 35
The Wren, 37
Ebola, 39
I Remember, 40
We are One Again, 42
Everything is, 43
Panbody Blues, 44
Songs of the Trader, 46
Conversations from Down Under, 47
Prosperity in Austerity, 48
Leave us Alone, 49
This is Who We Are, 51
The Raucous, 52
The Shots, 53
My Town, 54
Don't Leave Me Here, 55
Come to Me, 56
Growing up, Kortright, 57
Stand Up, 58
We're Up, 59
We're on Our Way, 60
It's On, 61
Let me Be, 63
I and We, 64
Tell Me, 65
I'm on my Way, 66
Temple Run, 67
In the Belly of the Mediterranean, 69

Blackness, 70
The Joy up the Hill, 72
Knowledge is Light, 74
Zindaba, 76
IMAT–Institute of Management Accounting and Tourism, 78
Wisdom Tree, 79
Bustik, 81
Airport, 83
Dudley, 85
I listened, 87
Happy, 89
Look at Me, 90
Because I'm a Woman, 92
It's All Before My Eyes, 94
My Firefly, 95
This Dust, 96
Babeng, 97

Endorsements

Abdulai Walon-Jalloh's *'Panbody Blues'* is the Mistress of the City

The collection of poems entitled 'Panbody Blues' by Abdulai Walon-Jalloh is a not too verbose dedication to his teachers and friends, and as a reminder to us of the kaleidoscopic nature of life. His 'Panbody Blues', is a small volume for what seems like a decade's work. Over a 100 pages, it could easily be overlooked on a shelf beside the collected work of other poets. Lecturer of Syntax, Walon-Jalloh attended closely to the textures and music of words. He is a poet who carried traditional poetic techniques like rhyme and meter forward into thoroughly modern poems that make us feel strong and optimistic. His poem 'The Loss' famously ends,

"Lighten up
To gain victory
And loosen up to lose defeat
As the brave falter."

Using overcritical and ostentatious metaphors and ironies, he reassures us to meaningful dénouements in just a few lines. The vitality of his poems is felt in its condensed nature and syntax. There are lots of metaphors to disclose greater truths. For example, in 'The Robin', and 'The Wren', the poet uses a bird's solitary flight as a metaphor to explain his loneliness, endurance, and sadness. Spectacular and situational ironies reflecting significant life events such as death, disease, and poverty are not rare in his poetry. A brief read of 'In Memory of the Fallen' gives us an example of a dramatic irony in which the fallen are unaware of the situation but the audience is not, as seen in the lines:

"Your purpled T-shirt on okada
your lifeless body across the streets."

In 'The Sun and the Palm-Tree', we see the poet's use of a situational irony in which both a character (the sun) and the audience are fully unaware of the implications of the real situation. Not until the last two stanzas did we learn about the final fate of the sun:

"The Sun, with sleepy eyes, replied, 'I want to rest. Take your quarrel elsewhere and leave me alone.

The Palm-Tree, gleefully and rewardingly reminded the Sun, 'Didn't I tell you that you will give in to sweet nature's call? Adieu!!"

By using ironies, Walon-Jalloh creates extreme suspense and even satire in his poems. He thus highlights, elaborates and expresses feelings and dispositions more commendably.

Likewise, the poet uses alliteration as an excellent analogy and with a marvellous sense of sound. His use of the "ck" sound in 'Guardians of the Earth' allows us to almost hear the clicking sound of the bird's beak itself. The way the words "-back" and "-neck" play in the poem is stunning, as the image they create is exact and elitist, thereby giving Walon-Jalloh the advantage to execute an imposing task.

The poet's use of similes too is remarkable. For example, in 'Blackness' we see such images as:

"Unable to breathe like fish out of water
There was blackness like charcoal at night"

Similarly, in the poem 'I Listened' the poet paints a picture of "Multitudes with outstretched tired palms like potato leaves in the dry season."

Grosso modo, the poet's approach is rather honest towards issues like religion and spirituality, marriage and divorce, friendship and peace, knowledge and learning, the past, the present, and the future. With a little bit of exertion, readers can associate to the major themes in his poetry. The poems tackle and settle conflicts proficiently by cautiously creeping through historical and cultural issues.

Interestingly though, I couldn't recognise a perfect three-line poem with seventeen syllables, written in a 5/7/5 syllable count lines of the traditional Japanese haiku structure. Nevertheless, three-line poems like 'Today' and 'Ice and Dice' accentuate guilelessness, strength, and honesty of expression as is typical in haiku-structured poems.

Similarly, I wasn't able to pinpoint an ideal limerick-patterned poem consisting of five lines wherein the first, second, and fifth lines must have seven to ten syllables while rhyming and having the same verbal rhythm. And the third and fourth lines having five to seven syllables, thereby rhyming with each other and having the same rhythm. The poems 'Everything Is' and 'This is Who We Are' stood out strongly with five lines but fall short of the same verbal rhythm.

Again, I may have failed to recognise iambic pentameter consisting of five sets of unstressed syllables followed by stressed syllables; a Shakespearean style. Generally, and to some extent, rhyme, meter, and order tend to follow similar patterns, while the content in each poem flows smoothly, broken down into readable stanzas.

I am with the impression that Walon-Jalloh wrote the poems because he wants to remind us of the psychedelic character of life, and its inherent challenges. Hence, his poems are filled with those recurring themes of religion and spirituality, marriage and divorce, friendship and peace, knowledge and learning, the past, the present, and the future. By and large, Walon-Jalloh's poems are a logical progression of thoughts and ideas as seen in the 'Binta' series. Most of his lines are simple, but work efficiently in their originality.

Perhaps this is why he is so good at writing in original ways about calamity. 'Absence Presence,' his emotional poem about Aminata Walmar Walon-Jalloh's death, becomes a brief meditation on a new experience of tragedy; his 'Ebola' speaks of that difficult era from the opinion of an apprised Greek refrain indirectly defying Aristotle's ideas about tragedy; and the poem 'In the Belly of the Mediterranean' suggests that the crossing from Africa to Europe is not really a story of tragedy at all but a dream of people selecting a more frightening but also more lovely environment.

Walon-Jalloh's poems not only handle difficulty; they also make something innovative of it. Let's contemplate, for example, this passage from 'Babeng,' the collection's last poem:

"It's lightning, thunderclaps and rains
Babeng zooms to and fro with outstretched arms over stall
Nature's beatings unstoppable and the deluge on the ground overcomes
We all fall to the ground to drink of a day's spell
Smiling Babeng reassures and our rock determination to triumph flagged
The wet un-housed chicken circle round the cock with the hen hurrying in from the outside
The sun has receded farther into the sky."

The subdued splendour of these lines makes the probability of being disregarded no longer feel so forbidding. What they say confirms the likelihood of this fate, but how they say it transforms the way that I feel with regards to it. The chance of being disregarded becomes related to a vision of a better future world, one without thirst or the memory of our sorrows.

In the collection as a whole, the genre is difficult to pinpoint, and hence the word choice to support it too. The collection has a geography as Robert Frost has New England, Abdulai Walon-Jalloh has Freetown and its enclaves, as seen in 'Panbody Blues' referred to as "skycrappers of Kroo Bay, Moa Wharf and Bomeh." In conclusion, I think he successfully gets his message across.

Bakar Mansaray, Ottawa, Canada
July 2017
www.mandingoscrolls.blogspot.com

Another showcase of the poet's mastery...

Panbody Blues by Abdulai Walon-Jalloh is another showcase of the poet's mastery to get the appropriate diction, in a successive manner, in the lines which form the various poems. This collection spans a wide range of issues and themes which have been expressed using various techniques.

The use of the Haiku pattern of writing makes the reader easily grasp the thoughts of the poet in each of the three line poems and this type of writing makes the collection intriguing and compelling to read. The use of a paradoxical title in the first poem shows Walon-Jalloh's deep passion for a beloved father or relative who, though dead and gone, still lives on the poet's memory.

As the reader goes through the poems, he is presented with a summarized narrative of the Ebola scourge in Sierra Leone. This inclusion of the Ebola poem brings fresh memories to Sierra Leonean readers who witnessed its occurrence between May 2014 and November 2015; that scourge devastated the country and brought it to a halt.

By the time the reader gets to the poem from which the title of the collection is derived, one is thrilled by the diction used and at the same time saddened by the succinct description of living in squalor which is common to many people in Sierra Leone and across the world as a result of poverty and the lack of some or all of the socio-economic facilities. In fact, the poem *Panbody Blues* is personified in the first line of stanza two and that clearly points out how makeshift structures are common in Serra Leone where the poet originates.

My dear reader, you have the greatest opportunity to peruse the interesting poems in this *Panbody Blues* collection and learn more from the illustrious Abdulai Walon-Jalloh who has undeniably done justice to this piece.

Prince E. A. J. Kenny is the Head of Department for Language Studies, Fourah Bay College, University of Sierra Leone and a PhD. Staff Candidate. He has also published plays, poems, reviews and short stories.

A literary Inspiration

Panbody Blues by Abdulai Walon-Jalloh can be considered as a 'Dancing and Seeking Memory' verses which whirl around the aspect of success, determination, consolation, benediction, supplication, pity, frustration, sacrifice, fear, mental power, parenting, mundane wishful thinking and care.

However, this solemn collection is an embodiment of our greatest fear as humanity not based on our inadequacy as persons, but rather our assumed powerfulness, powerlessness and viocelessness beyond imagination. This book of poetry can be perceived as a thought-provoking piece of literary work that sounds like a chirping bird's song of the old generation of idealist and the young generation of tech-savvy wealth seekers. The title of this book of poetry is rather shocking, reminiscing and probes a sense of enthusiasm in the reader to search for the understanding of 'our deepest ways to allay our fear in poetry', how poetry can be a social, cultural, political and economic therapy and what essentially the poet is talking about.

Walon-Jalloh's creativity in this second collection of his book of poetry remains outstanding, as it leaves the reader anxious to hear what comprises human beings, success, desires, sorrow and failures. The central rhythmic pattern in the book embodies the snail pace understanding of human nature and what we are meant for, our weaknesses, joys and potentials.

This book of poetry is a literary inspiration aimed at healing and empowering people in their daily lives. The poet was tolling poetic in choosing a title which resonates with his message. The title of the book is a reflection of the human nature in the sense that it reflects the weaknesses of people of failing to explore their potentials as a result of their background, status and social class.

According to the poet, the deepest fear within humans is not an individual problem or a situation by a group of people, but rather a situation faced by all people. This fear is unconscious and is demonstrated when people fail to maximize on their strengths.

As shown in the poem "The Loss", people are able to overcome this fear by maximizing their potentials. By so doing, they are not only able to liberate themselves, but also liberate others in society. The poem is written in the most inspiring and empowering manner. The first two stanzas of the poem have great wisdom and inspiration regarding human life and innate effort. The poem gives an incredible depth of wisdom which may be unavailable elsewhere. The poem is powerful and insightful in its totality.

Some of the poems explore deeply the polarizing nature of humanity. We are astonished by the fact that humans are entirely powerful beyond measure, brilliant, talented, gorgeous, and awesome; yet they do not exploit their full capabilities. Walon-Jalloh shares his received wisdom by reminding us that humankind's deepest fear is that we are powerful beyond limit.

Some of the poems are stanzaic and inspiring in the sense that they call upon people to work with diligence and utilize their power. Walon-Jalloh believes that playing small has no service to the world and also that shrinking or shying away is far less noble. These are powerful thoughts which provoke people to think and act big for the service of the world and others.

In the fourth and fifth stanza of The Loss, for instance, the poet reminds people about what they are meant for. He says that people are meant to shine and manifest since the glory of God is within them. This is inspiring and it reminds people of their untiring accomplishments in the world and how they can squarely face the possibilities of mature and fulfilled life.

The speaker's voice is slightly invisible throughout the poem, whereby he acts as an imaginary speaker. Abdulai Walon–Jalloh does, in a way, share his life experiences throughout the poem, with the use of an invisible voice or an imaginary speaker. Despite that he has used the first person throughout some of his poems. This is a powerful approach, which helps to draw the reader's attention to the conditions of the personas in the different poems within *Panbody Blues*.

Most of the poems start on a simplistic note, but however become complex as they progress and then end somberly or upliftingly.

Mohamed Bangura Lecturer and PhD Staff Candidate Department of Sociology and Social Work Departmental Examination Coordinator, Secretary General, Academic Staff Association (ASA) Fourah Bay College, University of Sierra Leone.

A mixture of moralizing motifs...

Abdulai Walon-Jalloh's recent collection of poems, *Panbody Blues,* is at its most basic, a mixture of moralizing motifs, presenting thought processes and subjects that are common place and a tone or rhythmic tempo that is light yet intense and dramatic. As befits the title, Walon-Jalloh weaves personal reminiscences, search for self, loss, worship and submission; earthly truths, undefined and paradoxical; power and deprivation, eulogies for the tainted, memorable edifices, cravings for unfulfilled dreams and neglected cultural tradition; deception caused by assimilation and deceit caused by self-aggrandisement, political greed and police brutality; segregation as a result of man-made rules; ode to poetry and its timelessness; the ever present nature of evil; plaguing diseases and penury, in-action of the preliterate; life as opposed to death, noise as opposed to the eeriness of silence; verisimilitude of fictional events; forlornness; forceful migration and its gory effects; seeming happiness of a typical African community; women and abuse; love tryst and spooning, etc. into the fabric of this all-round corpus.

The poems are mostly written as long sentences, mirroring perhaps the flow of thought and run-on nature of events as the poet experienced them in the 'Panbody'. Yet, Walon-Jalloh advertently (perhaps inadvertently) arranges the poems in such logical sequencing of subject and imagery—(The dead and dying: As mortals wreck untold grief on each other; deceit: Sisyphus blossoms...Receding cultural tradition: I'm Binta of the fair-complexioned race, a proud race of distinct beauty and perseverance rooted in deep communal spirit and religiosity; religious recitation followed after the TV was obeyed in the morning, prayers were offered and school swallowed us) assailing all our senses.

Reading the poems, Walon-Jalloh transports by the strong vehicle of his rhythms through rugged roads of both daily subjects and themes to safe destinations—some emotive, others traumatic and still others outright plain, spontaneous and natural. Take for example 'Absent Present', communicated as a third-first-person narrative, adopts various tones—serious, paradoxical, etc. Poems usually begin with personal to general reflections.

The settings in the poems are largely bleak befitting the personas in the poems—barren, edifices, dilapidated or common abodes, etc., and the accuracy with which Walon-Jalloh presents these details is impressive whether dealing with personal, inward subject or objective, outward matter. Like Larkin, Walon-Jalloh writes in both "his social and political attitudes" (Fahy: 1999, p. 205: *New Poetry for Leaving Certificate High Level: Exploration*) and he (Walon-Jalloh) is here to stay both as a poet and as a playwright worthy of note.

Philip Foday Yamba Thulla, Editor, Poet, Novelist and Lecturer, INSLACS Njala University, Sierra Leone

Absence Presence

A poem in sweet memory of Aminata Walmar Walon-Jalloh who departed for the great beyond on Thursday 7th June 2012

Verily into the cold nights, where mortals dare not,
You waded your small frame through the air;
Into the wet red mud pregnant with a chill,
Your frame lowered.
With static smile; you inspire
Living mortals—beat their chests in anger.
In seething reply you remain still
Within the confines of this supposed loneliness.
You rose into the sky in the midst of birds.

In a confused wonderment you behold,
As mortals, wreck untold grief on each other,
"Why?" you ask. And with cherubic gait
You are in the sweet embrace of eternal suspense;
And there you seem to proclaim: "Cry not brothers."
"Cry not brothers."
"Cry not mother." "Cry not mother."
"Cry not father." "Cry not father."

"Gaze into my eternal smile.
Let my wide eyes transfix you.
Allow my radiance to brighten your lives,
I'm among you, forever
In your heart I shall remain.
Celebrate my absence with my void in your presence."

Abdulai Walon-Jalloh

I'm Badrie

I'm Badrie
Of cedar country
In lion mountain
And statue of liberty.

I'm the moon
In a starry sky
Over limitless desert
Amidst universal colors.

I sleep and talk
Sit and read
Stand and eat
Relax and play.

Behold my move
Pronouncing my firmness
When heralding my presence
Layered through my gazes.

Again!
I'm Badrie
Of cedar country
In lion mountain
And statue of liberty.

The Loss

In falling you rise
In rising you fall
In failing you succeed
In succeeding you fail.

Why the fret?
Why the glee?
Oh! You are brooding!
Ah! In wild ecstasy!

It's all in the mix
Rise!
Fall!
Succeed!
Fail!

The claque
The mourners
The triumphant
The vanquished.

Lighten up
To gain victory
And loosen up to lose defeat
As the brave falter.

Abdulai Walon-Jalloh

Gɔd

Na yu de sev yu slev
Na yu de gi am ples
Bikɔs na yu lɛk in layf
Fɔ mek I bɛtɛ bambay.

Natin nɔ de te
Pas yu se
Fɔ mek I de
So duya wi de.

Kɔba mi ed
Lɛ bad fred
So wi go rɛdi
Fɔ rid yu wɔd.

So bad go rɔn
Gud go tɔn
Fɔ mek wi lan
Gɔd in Man Wan bambay.

The Truth

In essence
The presence
As conscience
The waitress.

It's short
For the strong
As increasing faults
Surely, will prolong.

The receding star
On the firmament
Falls from afar
Welcomed by earth.

Earthlings in amazement
When nature astounds
In continuous excitement
As puzzle abounds.

Configurations in complexity
Simplicity an aberration
As understanding a perplexity
With realism in explosion.

A world of simpletons
Overcrowded by turgidity
And clarity the reality
Yet Sisyphus blossoms in turbidity.

Power

Many long yet few get
Securing power, the game of futility
For the victor's laughter is ephemeral
As the next phase alights without warning.

You deceive too many
And a good number refuse to learn
As generation after generation plays out its end-game
Though for many your fetching qualities overwhelm.

Your presence within so many is like a pack of cards
You are the smoke that disappears
As salt vanishes within other condiments
The lasting fragrance lingers.

Your attraction
Man's fascination
Your tantalizing façade
Man's doom and salvation.

The Passing Stream

Oh! How wonderful you flow
Through shrubs and mountains
Across landscapes and glow
You snake and maintain.

Many a wishes you float across
In spite of the dry times
You fondle and caress
Across to distant lands and climes.

Your presence in my sight
A site relished
In spite of my angst
My being is refreshed.

Your passing
I regret
Yet rhyming
You relate.

Friends and Peace

You are never too far away
In times of sorrow you sympathize
During joyful moment you excite.

What a world of peace
If friends were forever
Whether in novelty or in monotony.

You are closest to my heart
In all I do you are uppermost
We are bound by an invisible knot.

A knot so slender
Yet wiry
And unending.

It's indeed a peaceful world
If friends abound
And foes in dearth.

The Arrival

With blazes of glory
And incessant wailings and kickings
Your arrival is announced
Caring and eager hands are outstretched.

Pomps and presents at your feet
In your honour everywhere
Unending issues dot your face
At every given moment.

In religious and school playgrounds
Your presence is glorified
Where every recitation is treasured
Reluctantly, parents see you grow.

In quiet and turbulence prayers offered
You bedazzle and amaze
In wondrous agility and exploits
For you are child no more.

Binta: The Abyss

Here I'm on my buttocks
palms landing squarely on the floor
wide-eyed, I search for the straws
with outstretched popped ears listening
when no sounds attend
teary-eyed, I look about
as passers-by move along listlessly
over my outstretched limbs
I eagerly wait, wait and wait
my flattened breasts running over my stomach
as my exhausted lips support sunken jaws
I'm Binta of the fair-complexioned race
a proud race of distinct beauty and perseverance
rooted in deep communal spirit and religiosity
a society closely knit by polygamy and sojourners.

Binta: The Anticlimax

Chasing law-enforcement officers
unyielding landlords and killing habits
overly ambitious friends who frequented night spots
sleepless central Freetown with well-lit streets
easy friends steeped in the primrose paths
with no worry for tomorrow or regret over yesterday
children of today spawned from the depths
crouching in tunnels and waterways
sneaking up on innocent bystanders
disguised noon-tide gamblers
and transformed night crawlers
visiting zombies in schools and centres
with unfettered spending sprees
visible in upscale Freetown, I's grounded.

Binta: The Pre-Anticlimax

A handsome body
represented by a perfectly sculpted face
approached our courtyard and my heart gave a lurch
he was the one in my dreams
my paralyzing heartbeats ceased as he approached
he was a first degree cousin living abroad
our eyes interlocked; my heart melted
if he'd wanted me he'd have succeeded
he enquired about our parents and I guided him
festivities followed as I was his and he's mine
Mamudu was living life on the fast lane
Mamudu a self-styled returnee
pregnancy after pregnancy followed disastrously
he melted in the early hours of Tuesday
on Wednesday I's officially divorced
I sat by the window and cried and then smiled
I'm free at last. It's good whilst it lasted.

Binta: The Climax

I'm the last in a family of nine
we'd everything going for us
a house as big as a palace
marshaled by three mothers
at the apron-string of our father
I's the most beautiful
blessed with a desirable body
fronted by mesmerizing eyes
a majestic height and long hair
always interfering with my sharp face
captained by a pointed nose and full lips
my hips sat prominently on my long limbs
as my fatty contents were disappearing fast
every male came calling as suitors
and my wicked and haughty denials frustrated them
I's at the height of my powers
though ignorant, foolish and petulant.

Binta: The Sun Sets

Father always returned in the evening
we sat round him under the pear tree
to listen to his anecdotes and complaints
he showered us with gifts and led us in prayers
our mothers prayed behind him
we dined together amidst laughter
religious recitation followed after the tv was obeyed
in the morning, prayers were offered and school swallowed us
father hurried to his goat store
and our mothers attended to the stomach and sanitation chores
my presence always caused a stir
that's why Wurrie always proposed
and my usual self disappointed him
Wurrie never gave up and I never relented
under the tree behind our house every evening
I ordered him to wait. Wait he did
my heart pitied him for he was poor.

Wurrie wept openly at my marriage
with total disregard, I took no notice
we went our separate ways and destiny claimed us.

Binta: The Dawn

Wurrie frequented our courtyard
and my mother sent him on errands
these were his ruses to set eyes on my person
I'd order him to the market, the well, the field
yielding Wurrie had a place in his heart for my person
my arrogant and big head missed true affection
humiliated, Wurrie offered to carry my bag
his friends ridiculed him, I took their side
Wurrie looked me up with watery eyes
I thought him crazy and odd
indeed, he never was but truly in love
I threw it all in the air
Binta and Wurrie lived worlds apart
as hearts were slowly moving towards each other
as I lay in my grubby room reminiscing.

Binta: The Sun Rises

A knock and a familiar voice called out
"Binta! Binta! Binta! I'm Wurrie."
"Why me?"
"I've come for you."
"I hate myself for being stupid and blind."
'You're mine.'
"You've always been my rescuer."
"What say you to my proposal?"
"I don't deserve you."
"Don't say that Binta, I must prepare for you."
"Come into my arms. My sweet love."
"So indeed the sun always rises."
"I'm Binta and he's Wurrie."

Tomorrow

We shall be on an even keel
though we may wish it differently
yet faith will reside in us still.

You will forgive our mindless generosity
though we shall cherish our present lack,
fate will unite us under a single roof of pity.

Now that our joys and sadness forgotten
and the embrace of the most High assured,
we can continue to prosper and soften.

Let's not regret our previous conditions
as there was a larger design for their happenings
thus the needlessness for endless petitions.

The fragrances and blossoms will nourish us
for the warmth of our Host shall inspire mankind
when beings and animal-kinds shall live in one pulse
as none is left behind
that will be tomorrow.

Yesterday

We were together
in the toughest of days
as time stood still in waiting without a bother.

There you were with us as one
you seem to have forgotten
but remember, when you wailed and closed up your tone?

As you lay abandoned in your mess
in the middle of the road—
when stray dogs and cats kept you company as you lay penniless.

Under the deluge stood your muddied self
aimless, unhappy, forsaken and alone
we gave you rest and hope in spite of yourself.

That was yesterday
when you were under the grinder
and we were your guides for the day
in the midst of lightening and rumbling thunder
again that was yesterday!

Today

You are at the top of your game as life favours you
we are at the nadir of our lives
and our beings and possessions are few.

When shall we see each other?
time is running out for us
though, yours is running in.

Your world is clockwork
ours is not time bound
and penury abounds in our luck.

Today our paths do not cross;
they used to crisscross, though
as we are constantly in a loss.

We want you to find us
though, you may be occupied.
we are not making any fuss
for we were once united.

Again, this is today!

In Memory of the Fallen

Inspired by the March 2017 Njala University students' demonstrations across the country

I'm elected and wealthy
I'm in power and powerful

My eyes see only the ballot
as my fingers hold the bullet

Your purpled T-shirt on okada
your lifeless body across the streets

I see my time hurrying near
my reign of fear unhinged

We bathe in party colours
colours in your veins and arteries

We shelter in your shade
shade with rootless facade

Your anger drowned by our ululations
as heaped platitudes on a painted shed

Hurry to your graves spent forces
until our till is filled

Wave your empty palms to us
with lack we shall fill

The FAlLeN shall rise never
yet in yore they will arise

Wipe your tears
pick up your battered selves

ThE FaLlEn will RiSe!

Geometry Set in Pain

your geometry set in pain
with dividers to keep us apart
compass of treasures
erasers of wrongs and pain
sharpeners of passions and chaos
angles by protractors off course
when rulers set the squares on fire
though the pencils' marks indelible
the tables in the set run amuck
when we are all in a geometry set in pain
must we all reverse into our sets of pain?

Ice and Dice

It's ice we sold
and dice we played
as mice ran amuck.

They were fleas we saw
when birds flew away
in the middle of the skies.

It's amens we chanted
when we felt slighted
as our fates were slanted.

Though we feasted
it never lasted
for we always fasted.

Where the sun blasted
under the palm tree we rested
thinking we're blessed.

Staying in front
was like being prompted
because it's not in us to take the brunt.

Those who remained were braver
for those at the helm were none the wiser
as providence has an appointment with all.

Eid

Eid is here
After Lamarana was there
fasting was observed
and charity was distributed
Ramadan and charity will go away
to come back another day
mankind shall celebrate the passing
yet angels will spend their time weeping and wailing
as everyday happenings are unhinged
so humankind will be unhitched
to plunge into their deepest abyss
He shall endeavour to make up for their loss
humankind do hope to experience another masterpiece
though it shall please Him not to grant their release
when many are about
most will go without
though happiness shall not long evade them
as He always guarantees peace of mind within their frames
in His Might they worship
as midgets in His ship.

Poetry

Ah! The ability to tame the stillness
The strength to steady uneasy calmness
When quarrelling thoughts burst forth
In wondrous amazement no spendthrift
Inured to paucity in the realm of plenty
As strained eyes trace a path in a lurch
Where eager fingers compete for connections
Because the trigger shall soon be on the move once again
Though fretting fate will ever deceive
Yet the tamer of the wild triumphs
Figures formed with words
Float everywhere like flying swords
When mankind in its folly err
The true poet poses in eternal truths.

The World in Parts

The world in parts
a part for the weak
another for the not-too-faint-hearted
one for the strong
still believe the world is one and fair
in spite of the parts?

Living it in the whole
never a time the world been one and fair
for inhabitants at the time
surely one walks the world
to amaze, weep, rejoice
depart between sunrise and sunset.

The footprints of time
left behind to behold
instruct across generations though few heed
the present a constant state of flux
interactions will carry the past
into the future.

Fragments of memories cohere
actions of mankind different times of reckoning
imaginings restore bruised hopes
flagging passions across the stretch
passions the breasts of mankind
balm for battered but not lost souls.

Panbody Blues

No wonder the world in parts
for those who can partake.

Brave Cowards

I come into the world
to stand up to injustices and iniquities

I love my gains
cannot go without them

Let me fly away to the comfort of and embrace
of lands with histories of social struggles

Struggles to which I contributed not
but will happily ensconce myself with that warmth

My pen, from afar, will etch out the ills of my home town
and not dare to stir up trouble

My lit up surroundings contrast with my drab world
from where my ancestral loins lay buried

Behold my paved and glassy ambience
mocking my pent up anger for my impoverished homeland

The electric candelabra
dwarfs my grandmother's kerosene lamp or pan-lamp

Manicured grassy plots flourish in my courtyard
defying my manure-ridden but barren plots yonder

Literati retreat, mass protests in reverse gear
grass root explosions for Hobbesian cravings.

The Sun and the Palm-Tree

"Have we met before?" the Sun said to the Palm-Tree
"Yes, several times have our paths crossed," the Palm-Tree replied.
"Oh! Now I remember," replied the Sun.
"And I think, our destinies are connected," the Palm-Tree retorted.
The Sun, shaking its head and shooting its chest forward confidently affirmed, "Hmm…whenever we meet tears and joys will surely go either way."

The Palm-Tree shook its head and said, "Indeed…so may tears and laughter follow us through the valley of deprivation and the primrose path."
The Sun, remorsefully, said, "is there a way to stop this so that our folks can just celebrate after our meetings?"
The Palm-Tree arrogantly remarked, "I don't think so because we are sworn enemies and the battle is to the finish."
The Sun, sensing that ground has been yielded unnecessarily, regained its composure and replied, "Well to the death then."
The Palm-Tree realizing its unwarranted boastfulness, remarked, "I think there could be a way out."

The Sun, surprised, though not completely, breathed heavily and slumped its chest and asked, "How?'"
The Palm-Tree, panting, narrated the ordeal of their folks who could not shelter under the limited cover of the palm fronds especially when running away from the intense heat-rays of the Sun, said "Reduce the intensity of your emissions."
The Sun, angrily replied, "But that is who I am. I must emit heat waves to nourish and perish life. Plants, humans and other organisms need me in order to grow and die. Even you require my rays in order to process your food. You see."

The Palm-Tree, noticing defeat, remarked quickly, "Well, why not decimate all of us and then have the spheres to yourself?"

The Sun, laughingly replied, "The world will be a boring place without you and the others. I am because you are and I'll be because you shall be. We are intertwined. Don't you get it? My ferocity is but a façade. A bluff. A front. I'll die if there is nothing to kill."

The Palm-Tree bravely replied, "You are not up always. At night you shall seek you repose and that will be the time I shall be out to seek your eclipse with the help of your cousin, the Moon."

The Sun, hardly audible, retorted, "Why are you telling me this, if you can do it?"

The Palm-Tree calmly replied, "The lonely star shall always wait for the night when your eyes are closed before it possesses the sky."

The Sun, shaking and moving from one point to the other, grunted, "I, Sun, shall never sleep because I don't want this to happen."

The Palm-Tree fleetingly enjoined. "You shall and will be asleep for it is nature's call to all of us to obey its dictates. Who are we to say no."

The Sun, with sleepy eyes, replied, "I want to rest. Take your quarrel elsewhere and leave me alone."

The Palm-Tree, gleefully and rewardingly reminded the Sun, "Didn't I tell you that you will give in to sweet nature's call? Adieu!"

Dublin

An Island wet, cold, clean, quiet, darkening skies, geriatric and soporific ambience
A determined city unwilling to lag is in pursuit of its known, liberating, oppressive counterpart across the border in the English Isles
Grassy, leafless trees and squawking seagulls and dutiful parents and marshalled children
Majestic mansions steeped in historic theology and shamed by modernity
It is a sunless afternoon with occasional brilliant shine and hurrying students and clergy
Frantic movements in trepidation or expediency or survival along shielded corridors and crafted gothic windows festooning medieval architecture
Of times embroiled in resistance and domination and freedom into protective cultural age for a sceptical race.

A race tainted and horrified by unreligious excesses and puritanical aggression
Twin cities in a divided country and a testament to oneness and mono-focal destiny
The underbelly of a union that is far away from the continent
A city of proud folks with an undying passion for culture and future identity
Gallant clergy with a big heart withstanding the crucibles of secularism and libertarianism
The City of Guinness and Whisky and Potatoes and Marches
Unyielding forces battling entrenched values coloured by religion, famine and migration
The City of cobbled roads from indentured labour and blood-stained hands and sweaty brows from mixed extractions.

The homogeneous jewel in the crown of Europe adjacent UK Isles in the middle of an ocean

What's next Dublin the land of the fiddle and strings and bass and drums?
Or the pursuant of convoluted dreams in brightly-coloured double-decked buses shall continue to lead the way into an anxious future that lies in wait?
A wait that will not be too long to be over on your paved roads and alleys to deliberately manicured and less-used lawns and gardens and other open public and private spaces.

I love Dublin City.

Guardians of the Earth

You White-back and Red-neck!
Why do you soar high up in the sky?
They say you weigh 7kg,
Some say you can grow up to 4ft,
Some believe that you can live for over thirty years,
What happened to your neck?
Why are you so dark or brown?

Hey, White-back and Red-neck, leave the carcasses alone!
You wash in rivers and streams after every meal.
You eat your food raw;
Entrails, ligaments and other softer body parts fascinate you.
Leave the garbage and dump sites alone!
Our skies are never complete without you.
You, who always provide the way,

They say you hover around food,
You are always closer to water,
Your neighbours are warm-blooded creatures,
You are seen around slaughter houses,
Dumpsites host you eagerly;
You reside in tall trees.
Longevity is attracted to you, guardians of the earth.

Hey, White-back and Red-neck, you are the conjurers;
We poison the habitat; you heal the world,
You bring life but we take it;
You show the way as we obliterate it,
You provide us the excuse to be happy but we make everyone, include you, unhappy,
You inspire the tired and lost way-fearer with your presence,

You are the conqueror of the African skies.

Hey, White-back and Red-neck, you are the wisdom of the ages;
You're the gods of the Ancient and Middle Ages,
You're friends of the skies,
You're mates of giant trees,
You're rusted friends of the carcasses,
You're the bringer of health and master of longevity.

The Robin

I'm not tall, neither fat nor huge.
I'm Robin, the midget bird.
I've a longish tail though my beak does stand out,
My wings and tail are darkish brown or black.
My two slender feet carry me easily,
Also, my bright brown or golden breasts or chest
pronounces me well.

I come in the morning to wait on tree tops.
When folks are eating and kids are bubbling.
Towards door knobs, I call my friends.
We wait for food to come through pan tops;
We wait for kids and elderly folks to go to class.

We are the Robin Hood of the forests.
Monkeys and squirrels take notice of our arrival.
Snakes and iguanas and dogs and cats and humans want us
for feasts.
Arks and herons don't delight us.
We fly and conceal our breasts between trees.
Across the floor in scores.
Humankind sees us as pests.

We the midgets rejuvenate the forests.
We are music to stillness.
Our numbers gleefully dot the skyline.
When we rain on rooftops.
We do scamper over little food hills outside your doors.
Children delight in our bird-hood.
We're the other half of nature.

Our numbers are fell by your snares and traps.
At times, we are soup.
Sadly, we're quarried by our vengeful cousins.
Humans put us in cages to delight their homes.
We are put in cells to serve as study objects.
In laboratories as test subjects.
But remember we're free as Robin Hood.

The Wren

You call out to me in the morning.
You've a squattish splendour with an agile gait.
Darkish brown and light brown colours adorn your body with an active tail on sharp feet.
Your wings are too short but can respond to motion.
You and your team wait on tree tops chirping at the top of your voices.

The brilliant morning sun bounces of your brown and dark feathers.
You always sit on the leaves and branches of our mango trees.
You always move closer to your target as the electric cable, and shrubs your halfway points.
With lightning speed from the shrubby flower,
You'll alight on your target and away to safety.

The overpowering sky does not overwhelm you.
Not even the giant masts and tree tops frighten you.
Your practised steps see you wait patiently for the right moment as you sit on the cable.
You're not perturbed by the eager kindergarten kids strolling underneath your gaze.
You wait and wait and wait and then to the leftovers on the floor and back to your safe spot.

The rich pickings on the heaps await your intervention.
Up on top of the electric cable you'll call out to your friends.
And friends in their numbers will heed and playfully wait for the moment.

You all alight on the heap to feast on food from yesterday and the heap of life is gone.
Your little swollen belies and high pitched twittering are testaments to your joy.

In motion in the air is the panoramic view we long for.
Up and up as free spirits shall always elude us.
Gigantic masts, tree tops, roof tops and shrubby tops we dream of.
Gazes on either side leave us in wonder.
Twittering and chattering astound us. We're jealous!
You, the little bundle up in the sky will manage our environment as you put smiles back on our faces.

Ebola

Who are you?
Why are you angry?
Where are you going?
Will you come back?

In the morning you are quiet
In the afternoon, very sprightful
In the evening, calm
Late in the night, quiet again
The night is quiet but you are about
The stillness lightens the mood
In the frenzy of your moment your bloodshot eyes,
Eyes that instil fear in no one in particular.

Invocations are in vain
Your essence appeals to me
Come I will
Stay I must
I am in your midst
Poverty, misery and greed are my forerunners
My presence can be muted
In state where plenty and discipline abound I lurk
Flourish, I may, when the conditions are right.

I Remember

I remember the forages into the woods
the steep climbs towards Quarry
the sweet descent from Mount Aureol
the glorious swims.

I remember the night outs
the eager and pained calls
journeys through cemeteries
the snares and hunts.

I remember the giant rats
the crickets of the undergrowth
the meows of the cats
the barks of the dogs.

I remember the never-ending matches
the unfinished narratives about movies
the angst of losing the Lotto stakes
the unrequited love.

I remember the yells and jells of friends
the thunder from the teachers
the noises from the markets
the sounds from emptied palm wine cups
the flaps of the palms over the twisting coins.

I remember the clucking sounds from the dice
the rattling from Bingo seeds
the taps from play cards
the clicks and smash from Targets Guns

the rings from the school and church bells
the Azan from minarets
the clings from breakfast and lunch plates and cups and spoons
the swishing blankets over tired bodies
I remember.

We Are One Again

Beautiful eyes or handsome eyes or sheer magic
you stand before me
in all your splendour
those rows of milk teeth
glare at me with blinding flashes
your pink lips and flappy ears astound.

Midgets beauty you are
when you play under my gaze
I feel fulfilled and hopeful
the babbling wet lips and clumsy steps
a running nose and a playful spirit.

The outdoors receive you so well
when you pound the steps
my heart misses a beat
with Angel's assurance recline
with full belief in the divine
a design hung over you when you are about
as you seek the air of the outdoors.

You always take me along
in my heart of pumped up heart
your image and touch linger
those chubby cheeks and stubby fingers
ready to trace a line in the sand
a line we both shall walk
hand in hand when we walk into the horizon
we are one again.

Everything Is

Is this your touch?
Are these your gazes?
Where is this chocolate smell coming from?
Which air is coming my way?
Yours, indeed!

I remember your hands back in the day
I can see your eyes as I look across the sea
I am feeling you with my nostrils
my body is cooling off as your air comes upon me
you are, indeed!

Let's walk hand in hand into the eclipse
let's look into each other's eyes
let's savour each other's odour
let's sample each other's breath.

Buoyed up kites in the sky
joyous ducks afloat in the pond
unhinged leaves and branches dancing to the sweet breeze
herrings and tilapias swimming merry in the sea
the brilliant sun and comfy palm tree.

This touch liberates
these eyes inspire
the fragrance soothes
the air enlivens
everything is!

Panbody Blues

The rusty and grainy ambience
that clatters and clings when rats and roaches travel
the *patapata* of rain drops
the oozing air through the myriad inlets
the streaming lights follow from the outside
haunting human noises
card boards paddings and plastic ceiling serenade
damp and heat pile on each other
the moist and sweat greet well
on the outside when inside
at the top when below.

Panbody, the mistress of the city
skycrappers of Kroo Bay, Moa Wharf and Bomeh
the beginner of stories
the final destination for the less-fortunate and distraught
the joy and sadness of the multitude
the bane of city planners and policy makers
a sorry and confusing ubiquitous object
saviour of the hard pressed
scorn of the successful
master of claustrophobia and propinquity
the glittering giant of the outdoors.

Sky-high dreams
visions of wealth
on sweaty shirts
hopes of travels
hopping rats feet
majestic mansions

Panbody Blues

fragile foundations
education conquests
book-less spaces
beautiful women
empty stomach.

The panbody blues ...

Abdulai Walon-Jalloh

Songs Of The Trader

Wares on my head
purse to my waistline
slippers pounding the rocks
long distances to cover.

Wares on my tray
customers very far away
money in a tight corner
time does not matter.

Monies in my purse
sperm in my tubes
hearts skipping a beat
visits to the charlatan.

My life before me
a lonely tiring journey
why didn't I see
with my charge alongside?

No longer mindful of the due collector
no longer heedful of that parental advice
no longer the innocent child of then
I'm now a gown child woman.

Conversations From Down Under

They've said all yet again
we continue to listen.

They'll say it all over again
we shall listen yet again.

The ninety degrees about face turn
in the summersault of delight.

Tears continue down our cheeks
deprivation rolling up our sleeves.

Back pains will haunt us to the grave
in backward progression we rolled up bliss.

But from the lower frequencies
we rise and possess.

Again, they too will say it all over again
and we'll listen to them all over again.

Prosperity In Austerity

Change is come
rise and rejoice.

Hope is here
participate and dance.

Reforms abound
change retreats.

Transformation in prints
results in shadows.

Sleaze galore
back-foot justice.

Scourge unchained
prosperity barrenness.

Guaranteed austerity
dictions flourish.

Winning ballots
losing victories.

Leave Us Alone

Where were you when Pedro visited?
Where were you when the Manes invaded?
Where were you when the jihadist stormed?
Where were you when the Province was established?
Where were you when the Colony was rammed
down our throats?
Where were you when the Protectorate was proclaimed?
Why did you betray Bai Bureh?
How was it that Chiefs were silenced?

How was Independence gained?
How comes One-party was declared?
How was it that Ndorgbowusu gained prominence?
How did NPFL cross over?
Why is perfidy doing well?
Why is education in the backburner?
Why are women folks still in the wings?
Why are the queens with no queendoms?

Why are we killing each other?
Why the scourge?

Leave us alone!
and not sport
and not eat well
and not job
not drink well
to go a-flooding
to go a-taxing
to not protect incomes
to not tour, sing, draw, sculpt, carve, act, read and dance

We are tortoises' shells
baboons' bottoms
the soles of the feet
the sun that rises, shines and burns daily
the sturdy, shady and prickly palm tree
the yellow light
the rolling bouncy
the cooling shade.

This Is Who We Are

The commodities of slave owners
bodies deep in the Mediterranean
vessels in the desert
sponges of emotions
fodders of war.

We come in all sorts
teary-eyed
watery nose
hallowed ears
wild hairs.

Out in the open
within closed spaces
they define us
not in our mould
but in their own.

This is who we are
the moon in the sky
the sun that shines
the stars that twinkle
that wind coming your way.

This is who we are
emboldening the age
soaking up the sludge
bouncing back from the fall
gatekeepers of the future
memory cards of generations.

Abdulai Walon-Jalloh

The Raucous

The raucous is about
Let's sustain it all over
But the grave; quiet place.

The Shots

You, calling the shot
For so long on this our planet
Life's short, indeed!

Abdulai Walon-Jalloh

My Town

I really love this town
It's in my heart and head
I'll take it along.

Don't Leave Me Here

Take me along with you
Your journeys are mine in yours
You and I'll journey.

Come To Me

I'm still waiting
Don't take too long to come
Time is limited here.

Growing Up, Kortright

Growing up at Kortright
Acting up like never dying
Living it forever.

Abdulai Walon-Jalloh

Stand Up

Stand up always stand up
Don't stand down for no one
The key going forward.

We're Up

Indeed, we're up
No down, down there for us all
The sky is high up.

We're On Our Way

We're on our way
to witness the joke
the joke at our expense.

We're on our way
to partake in the circus
a circus on our persons.

we're on our way
to drink peppered water
a way to calm nerves.

We're on our way
to listen to the gang
the gang over us.

We're on our way
to behold the parade
the parade that is us.

We're on our way
to see ourselves
ourselves, we.

We're on our way
to meet up with them
meet, we did.

We're on our way
to shock them out
out, they did.

It's On

It's on in the tabloids
the weekly and daily screams.

It's on in the airwaves
the throaty battles.

It's on on TV
the controlled gestures.

It's on in Ataya bases
the never-ending tirades.

It's on in the living rooms
discussions topical.

It's on in taxes, podapodas and buses
tales of tribulations

it's on on okadas
the maze existence.

It's on in the markets
the grinding toll.

It's on in mosques, churches and shrines
the daily diatribe and salvation.

It's on in schools and university
the anxiety and weariness.

It's on in farmyards, cinemas and hospitals
the charades and mirages.

It's on!

Let Me Be

Though 'm batter'd and down
rise, I shall one day like a clown
that day together
we'll soar to gather
so let me be to be happy with a frown.

Abdulai Walon-Jalloh

I and We

A universe so vast and fast
a life so dynamic with a blast
an end so nigh
I breathe a sigh
we climb so high fast with a blast.

Tell Me

I'm ready to listen to your history
listen to your blasted life in story
story in your image
lines of humanity a page
tell me, tell me a page of a caged lorry.

Abdulai Walon-Jalloh

I'm On My Way

Wait for me but I'm not on my way
I'm running to nowhere for me to sway
issues aplenty here
no distance shared
but penury gained to lose a tear for a tray.

Temple Run

To the memories of our beloved brothers and sisters perishing in the desert and the Mediterranean in order to get to Europe

Like the mosaic we are drawn
The desert sands hold our footprints.

In stops and gaps we sail past
The air will echo our tales.

At oasis we dream for more
Under palm trees we long for calm

At night we run for the temple
The starless sky always shows the way.

In bandits and cut-throats, we trust
Our homes treat us no less.

We wait for the right tide
Sail in the next dinghy.

The lights beyond
The snow yonder
The coast guard over
The jails across.

We trade places like one possessed
In deaths and abyss, we plunge.

Young faces
pretty voices

angelic screams
devils' roar.

We plunge to cross to die to live
the chasm we embrace. It's our Temple Run.

In the Belly Of The Mediterranean

To the memories of our beloved brothers and sisters perishing in the Mediterranean in order to get to Europe

In the belly of the Mediterranean
Our sons and daughters wail and flail for help
Calling out in the chilly nights for the hand of hope
They are food for the creatures and fossils to the seabed.

Your laments and anguishes left behind too huge for tears
In small dinghies and under the spell of con artists you kick yourselves to hope
The lights from across yonder can hardly shine for all of you, yet you embrace death.

I wonder what the story below looks like
A thousand feet below the surface
Wicked darkness envelops your beings as predators prey on your carcasses
In our beloved hearts you post despair and forlornness.

It is just a trip for the good life
With uniformed men and women on the other side waiting
Eager and greedy beings on this side urging
Whilst the spirit within explodes for the uncertainty.

Blackness

To the memories of our fallen brothers and sisters in the Mediterranean Sea hoping to run to better lives in Europe

I'm crushed to the sides of the dinghy
Unable to breathe like fish out of water
My head in reverse angle viewing the phalanx from the sides of my neck
I recall my coming, in my dreams, as my parents watch my head burst forth with mother's blood
My back hurts as my spine heavy from the strain coming from the shove.

Voices urging, hands flailing and eyes careening for more space
I can hear my siblings falling over me in our Panbody during the night for valuable space
Seagulls and flamingos and vultures overhead wait for our motionlessness I still cannot straighten my neck
I recall, in my dreams, sucking at my mother's tired breast smiling we both did
The dinghy kept racing on at snail speed and tortoise agility with the cunning of a chameleon.

My neck heavy and fingers numb as feet freeze
I recall the Harmattan in December and January as I lay groggy in our Panbody
I hope to get across and call back home to calm their anxieties
I look into the dead deluge and me thinks I'll never reassure them

Panbody Blues

Their torture will continue but my agonies and dreams will plunge with me into the sea.

Beautiful sea with death everywhere
Down the dinghy goes and my neck hurts no more
My blood supplies restored
My eyes filled with salt water
As my throat and lungs burst at stress point.

There was blackness like charcoal at night
I think we are going under.

Abdulai Walon-Jalloh

The Joy Up The Hill

The joy that is up th' hill
I see you clearly in my mind's eye
the tarred footpath going up the winding way
up there where my cogs are fashioned
the sleepy walks to the bastion of forgers.

I see the red earth from whence we came from our Maker
strewn in front of the incomplete u-shaped edifice
the land of Joe Cole, Coker, Neale, Lebbies, Zainab, Brima,
Zoker, Halowell, Dove-Edwin, Longstretch, Thorpe, Bitty,
Kallon, Ballay, Kargbo, Kallay and all
I remember the 7 am to 12 noon and 1 pm to 5 pm sessions.

I recall the climbs to Mount Aureol in search of students' leftovers and wild fruits
the swims at Quarry, Kakaswamp, Kalasona and Florigusta Farm
the quest walks through the Kissy Road Cemetery to Coknat Farm
the swims at Kissy Brook and Dam and Colbot
the Swimming Challenges at Gutters 1, 2 & 3 after the duel at Race Course Cemetery.

The eager walks to Starco Cinema for the second shows
spelling contests and pranks during examinations
the intense class rivalries during tests and examinations and lunches from the school feeding programme
the hot khaki sticking to our backs and naked feet crunching repeated miles to and from the joy that is uphill
the window shopping at Bata the shore store; marvelling at

stylish, rugged but dependable foot wears with little hope that they will ever adorn our battered feet.

The early morning walks with my kosang and lachiri[1] mixed and ready for the morning break in my finger-stained bag over my back before mouth-watering and lip-licking friends
my fingers never stopping to trace the contours of the plastic containing my morning joy
my parents hurrying me to Ginger Hall after the morning Quranic recitations
colleagues and my best friend joining me at the foot of the hill to the joy that is uphill
passing and waving jaramas[2] to uncles, cousins and aunts along the way.

The thrills of promotions and the frustrations of repeats
the anxiety during soccer matches and late evening sojourns from extra classes
the preparation for the public exams and the day itself at BJMS
the farewells and the embrace of the next challenge
the extra bonus in the joys of the Melbourne Soccer League and its giants

UMC Ginger Hall, the joy that is uphill.

---

[1] 'Kosang and lachiri' is a type of food made from cows' milk or dried non-fat milk and powdered corn mixed with sugar or salt or both
[2] 'Jarama' is a Fula Language greeting similar to 'hello'.

Knowledge Is Light

I remember you now as I'm climbing
the citadel on the mountain in the east-end
acacia-covered paths heralded by fine red pebbles and gnawing
our young feet found their way to your warm embrace at the top-end.

Your presence on the hill is the bus ready to move
windows and panes with locks as pupils ready to shove
fresh bluish and greyish or is it pinkish clouring provide the hues
with hope for the bell to announce the task at hand for the day's throes.

Yes, you are the light to the darkest paths and nimble minds with the source
you overlook the midget surroundings below like a Colossus
oh! you are Pegasus the flying wonder
the eerie young upstart neighbour of Laboramus Expectantes below yonder.

Your sister to your other side relishes your presence
as you stand in the way of Kuntolor and downstream yonder and their essence
ah! The friendly neighbours downstream our school for the differently able in other ways
of course, the cattle herders' delight in the foothills by the motor-ways.

The light in the storm never ceases
The will of undeterred teachers, minders and pioneers in attendance seizes
the flagship of Islam
the wonder of the east.

The joys of parenthood
you are who we are to be not in the hood
we were who you had been
the present, the nourisher on the keen.

Zindaba

The multitude of the east overlooking the seafront
Where eager and flux minds in awe are shaped to comprehend
Ways of the world and the Messiah's message
Shall open their eyes and minds to the closure and fulfilled ways
The hunger will and darkness will give way to truth and mercies
These tidings have found their ways to every corner
In spite of the number the many more now seek the way to truth.

Size rules
Many accept
Everywhere conquered
Message reinforced
Truth connects
Mercies received
Fulfilment galore.

Teachers from Asia genuflect to serve
The moon and the star obey
The sun possesses the sky
Knowledge multiplies in bounds
The seeds having been planted
Grow, they shall in the wilderness
Become the children of the Mahdi.

The seal shall never be broken
The message more perfect

Conquests solidified across the world
Faith strengthened in mankind
Truth long lost now proclaimed
In harmony we all walked
Zindaba, Ahmadiyya comes to serve and to serve forever.

IMAT – Institute of Management Accounting and Tourism

It is a child of the mind
Borne out of a necessity to serve
In the midst of littleness and scarcity
Hopes provided for the half-way aspirers.

New beginnings and new boundaries to conquer
You have grown to leviathan proportions and the envy and respect of many
The globe is your stage and the mind is your ultimate challenge
What better way to galvanize when spirits are low.

You never retreat in spite of the opponents
You modify your ways to square up to challenges
You convert impediments into stepping stones
Heights do not frighten you one bit.

Diversity and collaboration are your hallmarks
As you grow from strength to strength with a relentless drive and passion
With little resources yet strategic in vision and quick to act
Always ready to learn, deploy and harness best minds.

You've spread your tentacles across the globe
As you're the toast of Presidents, Ministers, Parents, Employers and Learners
IMAT the brainchild of Amadu, the outlaster of centuries and conqueror of dominions
You are the tortoise' back, the baboon's bottom, the soles' desperate feet and the Mount Bintumani

Wisdom Tree

I'm an old man sitting in front of Davidson Nicol
I'm the first gentleman you will see coming down from the Airport
some see me as a perfect circle and some don't
others see me as an imperfect triangle but some believe otherwise.

Generations have passed through me
yet my location and size remain the same
over the years I've been elevated from the ground
paint or whitewash, concrete seats and posters have blinded my true being.

Most of you see me as the convener of never-ending debates
others see me as the source of wisdom as my leaves ensnare and overwhelm
to some I'm the mid-way point to bottled or pent-up pleasure
the less daring will consider me a nuisance because they don't want to be challenged.

The famished and the filled exchange trophies under my gaze
laughter and tears I do entertain
during times of joy I receive brutal battering
my tree is sometimes assaulted by overzealous hungry folks.

During the rain, I'm the half-way temporal transit zone
in the dries my shade attracts reluctant and tired journeying folks
my face is sometimes blinded by the oppressive bills and inscription

underneath, creatures gnawing at my entrails wanting to come out.

The shouts from my abode can be heard way up and way down
the weight over me is heavy but I'm ready to carry it with me
mongrels and cats and ground pigs do glorify me when you humans are away
the wind and filth are unsparing of my essence.

I'm wise King Solomon
on the mines of Sheba
with the depth of Kasila and the bravery of Bai Bureh
and the age of Methuselah.

I'm Samson
the Chameleon King
patron saint of King Cobra
with the stretch of the lizards and eyes of the birds.

I shall remain the Wisdom Tree
The sage of Mount Aureol
The bastion of Fourah Bay College
That incorruptible and indefatigable platform.

Bustik

I can see you clearly in my mind's eye
of the days when we eager-eyed and wonder-filled
when Professors adorn you every corner
and by the Library's backside you relax
your presence is emboldened by your sister, Mary Kingsely
whilst you front visage beholds the University House
you are the half -way point to lecture rooms and the 'Airport'.

I like them days when you'll sit me to idly while away the time
in-between lectures
I turn my back on you to exit your temporary hold
a hold so sweet yet demanding
we all squat or stand on you to listen to speaker after speaker
as minds are won and lost
the big majestic mango tree is your centre and shade to all
while overzealous drivers violate your peace of mind.

Today, banks and the Obelisk are also your neighbours
sands and stones and water tanks your occasional intruders
some on the library fire escape to have a bird's eye view of
you and beyond
everyone loves Bustik
the calmer of nerves
the opposite to profuse sweating
the soother of nerves.

Splendid display of beautiful bevies and sprightful lads
the cover of lovers and nocturnal wanderers
the attraction to mongrels and twittering birds
the magnet of pelted stones and shedder of leaves

the giver of the sweet pulp juice that lingers long after the parent disappears.
a beautiful garden beckons but your loyalists resist preferring you
it is a wonderful world when the sun and the moon brighten over Bustik.

Your surface paved and unpaved provides the real feel
raised one-sided embankment provides the lure for searching eyes to entangle
as a world is provided for future engagements
the panache, the egos, the conceits and the attitudes all on display
the haves, have-nots, near-do-wells, the near-not-do-wells and creatures underground
will have their stories to tell though listeners reluctantly attend
this is Bustik, FBC USL. All are welcome. Let's learn.

Airport

I land Concordes and Airbuses
don't underestimate me
I'm the transit point to the ladies L. H. and Beethoven
eager young men blight my person with little respect shown

My runway runs to infinity
embarkation and disembarkation points loosely littered
I do have lounges and check in zones
with several terminals to my name.

My backside, today, is a disgrace
but my arrival centre is always sought after
taxiloads of Concorde payloads
bikeloads of Airbus deliveries.

With my eager marshals in green uniforms
which terminate into well-earned boots
supported by plastic truncheons
Chinese whistles and discarded American baseball hats

Today I boast a solar light
plastic, wooden and metal recline to my admirers
like the busy bees I receive inflows and outflows
lovers are not spared.

Without me no Fourah Bay
with me, the bakery and cafeteria and Third World are assured
look at my newcomer, Airtel Kiosk
you will never leave me behind because I'm locked in your brains.

Abdulai Walon-Jalloh

I'm a fixture at Fourah Bay just as the sea is to Kroo Bay
just as the stopper is to the bottle so am I to Fourah Bay
come let's celebrate
as we march on into the future.

Dudley

My feet come a-pattering
when my voice lowers and ebbs
with hand in pocket
peanuts with shells fall off my mouth.

With arm dangling to falling point
with weighty bag as heavy as the elephant's belly
grudgingly takes me aground
I stand my ground and forge on.

My doubly-lensed specs
hanging from a prominent nose
with ears attuned to scrutiny
never missing the hissing radio.

With students am at ease
their confusion dispelled
with wonderment they gawk
as year's span on a piece of paper.

Too many accolades follow me
yet no close family abides with me
a loner I am
though with books am game.

Always warmed up for the livid banter
I watch May Park lose and win
with undifferentiated suits
I'm about as free as a bird in the sky.

Colleagues know me not

Yet on me the rumour mill is active
Falsehoods at breakneck speed
My person is calm.

I outclass many
I outwit many
I outachieve many
yet they know not.

I'm the tortoise shell
the mystery cats' horn
the beard of the he-goat
Yet they see me not.

I Listened

I saw the commotion and heard the din
In the midst of the loss and hopelessness
I listened, waited and heard
I saw boys and girls play under the trees and run over fallen trunks
I behold the decrepit hollowness wallowing freely
Yet I listened

I heard the call to empty dances and rhythmless songs
I saw boys and girls hold on to empty promises
And adults with savaged facades offering hopes to the oppressed multitudes
Multitudes with outstretched tired palms like potato leaves in the dry season
A season of exaggerated movements and bottomed out bases
I saw folks dance the usual dances of forlornness and circular reasoning

I listened as hopes fly through the roofs
Roofs containing bitter souls from betrayed yester years
Rallied by the new songs belching from revamped stereos
I saw the measured responses from the citadel of hope and joy that is up the hill
They listened patiently to overworked tales of future splendor and self-empowerment
I saw it all unravel in front of my eyes, eyes that know it too well

I listened to the fall of withered leaves falling to the ground
I saw the drums and flutes play out monotonous ditties
While bevies and lads jump into the air to impress

I look back and shook my head knowing that the battle will be won and lost
The vanquished and triumphant shall walk work the same space till the next rounds
Nonetheless, I listened, heard, saw and looked into the horizon with tearfully joyous eyes

Happy

This is morning and the birds are up in the sky
Doors are opening and kitchen fires running races through rooftops
Elderly feet crushing leaf-covered paths into the forests
Stream-sides invaded by women and children for the early morning ritual

This is afternoon and measured voices dominate the landscape
When tamed voices follow cues from *karamakohs* (teachers)
Under the *barray* (chief's court) the chief issues out pronouncements
Whilst the earth is uprooted by violent unyielding hoes at the behest of practised grips

This is evening and the roost is returning home
Hoes, cutlasses and axes fall to the ground
Happy feet run over the courtyards as the *barray* closes down
Tantalizing smoke traces beautiful courses into the evening sky

We gather round raging fires in the cold night under a starry sky
Our eyes on the *igbakos* (wooden spoons) as the surface on plates transform into piles of joy
Our washed hands dip greedily into the mounds of joy as our impatient mouths wait for action
Happy are we under the watchful eyes of guardians

The stories begin in earnest until the eyes and filled stomachs conspire to overcome
Fires are out and doors are closed
Young ones laid properly and covered
Whilst elders whisper late into the night.

Look at Me

I fought in three battles and did not ask why
I fell in ditches and took the bullets for my leaders but did not ask why
I endured hunger and lack in the name of my leaders and did not bother one bit
I aged over the years in front of my leaders' gazes but did not ask why
I threw stones, hopped onto speeding vehicles, hid in trenches and intimidated my neighbours for my leaders but did not ask why
I lay in gutters to waylay my opponents and divert course for my leaders but did not ask why.

We rushed to rallies and abused each other in the name of our leaders and we did not ask why
We fought and killed each other in the name of our leaders and never asked why
We were arrested and released just to serve our leaders yet we did not ask why
The battles were won and lost just for the sake of our leaders yet we did not question why
We stood by and watched eagerly as posts and commissions were shared all in the name of our leaders yet we never questioned
We withstood unlimited tenures of plenty and penury all in the name of our leaders yet we did not ask why.

Yet, today, we wonder why we are who we are
We allowed ourselves to linger in the shadows hoping for flashes to rush upon us

Panbody Blues

Waited on our leaders to dine and wine whilst we whine and wimp
We are who we are because we were never who we ought to have been
We will never be who we are supposed to be because we are never who we are supposed to be
Look at me the spurned, scorned, shunned, taunted, torn, tormented and yet I were, am and shall be.

Because I'm A Woman

They don't send me to school
because I'm a woman

they force me through circumcision
because I'm a woman

they marry me early
because I'm a woman

they hurry me to the stream to fetch water
because I'm a woman

they put me in the kitchen to toil as a wife
because I'm a woman

they put me in the wings to serve in the women's wing
because I'm a woman

they put me in chairs to sit and do nothing as the cheerleader
for the chairlady
because I am a woman

they make me a queen without a 'queendom' to serve as their
mammy queens
because I am a woman

they make me Gender Minister
because I'm a woman

they make me deputy
because I'm a woman

they put me in markets and on the streets to hawk wares
because I am a woman

they make me First Lady
because I'm a woman

they put me through nursing
because I'm a woman

they deliberate and decide on my behalf
because I'm a woman

they beat me to pulp
because I'm a woman

they rape me
because I'm a woman

they take away my property and children after my husband's death
because I'm a woman

they marry me off to another man after my husband's death
because I'm a woman.

It's All Before My Eyes

The Range Rover Sports, four-by-four Four-wheel drives
Zooming past me into oblivion
The majestic splendour on hill tops and along paved roads
The manicured lawns and serenaded gardens keeping mansions away from the public eye
The leafy pools and balconied luncheons on the seafront
Gravity-defying high-rises on once public spots
Cheap and affordable public schools now-turned expensive unaffordable private spaces
The many created jobs for the boys and girls boasting only of handful staff
Farming that is office-based and boardroom-oriented
Increasing death-fields and receding playing fields
Dust-biting state enterprises and phantom jobs
Brutal takeovers sans liabilities
Widening web of schemers and profiteers around the Lagoon of Plenty
An opposition tearing itself to pieces before the race has even begun
Pyrrhic chameleon developments
Trophy-less election victories
It's all before my eyes.

My Firefly

It's night for us to be about
In the darkness of the stalls we stalled
We waited for the right time to tangle bright
Crazy horns and hurried labourers minded us not
You'll come into my arms with sweet tidings tickling my ears
In eager embrace and sparkling eyes did we melt into each other.

Your musical murmurings
The message tales of escapades
Wily ways to impress my reluctant in-laws
I see you burn tall in the night up into the starry sky
Excitement written all over your face as your cheeks blossom
We refuse to acknowledge anything anywhere at the time of the fireflies.

We see each other in the dark
Not even mindful of the vengeful flies feasting below
Our feet move from one spot to the other hoping to prolong the moment
Time flies, darkness thickens, dampness creeps up on us yet our focus steadied
Firefly you are, the dreamy way to airy path will steady us both as voices far come calling
Tell me you were worth the pain as I do know it's worth the drama and pain within the stalls
Firefly in me by my side in the cover of darkness under a starry night sky was worth the starring.

Abdulai Walon-Jalloh

This Dust

This dust under my feet
Strewn all over in front of my gaze
In the air and on leaves and trees
Dust from the undergrowth
Jetted to the surface by relentless shovels.

I wave my hand to drive you away
Yet you gain entry into me
Pulverising my eyes, nostrils, ears and mouth
The wind is an accomplice to your unruliness
I continue to fight you off.

Dust of the underground
Mixed with gore, bones, tissues, sinews, hairs and ligaments
The trace of a bygone era
Home of muted generations with no extra
Up in the air you float to greet and bade farewell at the gate.

We take a piece of you along to our homes
Pieces of yester generations in quieter times
We hurriedly wash you off with unpractised steps
With laughter you behold our cherubim attempts
You abide inside our beings.

This dust the colour of our skin
Yes, the source of our creation
Recipients of our beings
Nourisher of life and things
This dust the anchor of life.

Babeng[3]

A practised and routine step
The hovel is not space enough
'I must reach the sun'
Though it's night-time
Flip-flops scattering dust around
Reaches out to Neneh[4]
Babeng's touch.

Mount Aureol standing firm behind us
The Atlantic Ocean cuts us off from the front
Caught up in the din of the day
Sweat, tears and creaking bones
Genuflections at intervals and about-faced meanderings
A nokawako[5] topped by a grasping cap
Babeng is loose upon the multitude to inspire, calm and awe.

It's lightning, thunderclaps and rains
Babeng zooms to and fro with outstretched arms over stall
Nature's beatings unstoppable and the deluge on the ground overcomes
We all fall to the ground to drink of a day's spell
Smiling Babeng reassures and our rock determination to triumph flagged
The wet un-housed chicken circle round the cock with the hen hurrying in from the outside
The sun has receded farther into the sky.

---

[3] The Fula fond word for 'father'
[4] The Fula word for 'mother'
[5] A type of Fula dress i.e. an overflowing African gown for men. It is called the 'bubu' in some other parts

Abdulai Walon-Jalloh

The starry night sky
Chirpings from the undergrowth
Retiring steps retracing the journey home
Barking dogs and meowing cats
Closing stalls, bundled wares and filled up warehouses
Innocence spreads across the land
Mountains meld into the ocean

Babeng!

www.ingramcontent.com/pod-product-compliance
Lightning Source LLC
Chambersburg PA
CBHW032139040426
42449CB00005B/318